Vasectomy: What To Expect So You're Not Expecting

Written by Matt Bonatti
Illustrated by Mike Schmidt

When you don't want to have babies
And now it's all just fun
You've got to find a way
To put a safety on your gun

There are condoms and the pill
You can pull out and take your chances
Or you could abstain completely
From those horizontal dances

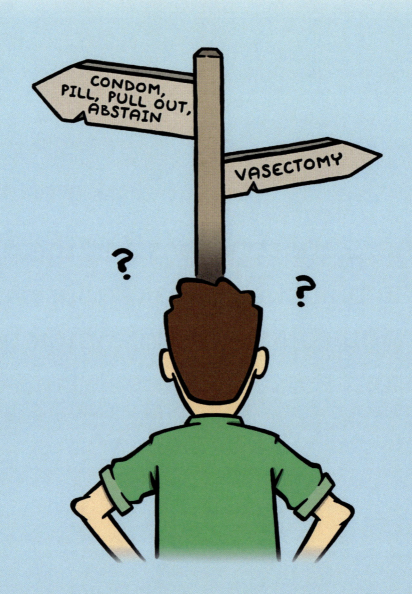

But there's still another option
Just listen and you'll see
You could go right to the source
And get a vasectomy

Your swimmers will be blocked
The pipeline will be closed
No more soldiers in your army
No more DNA in your hose

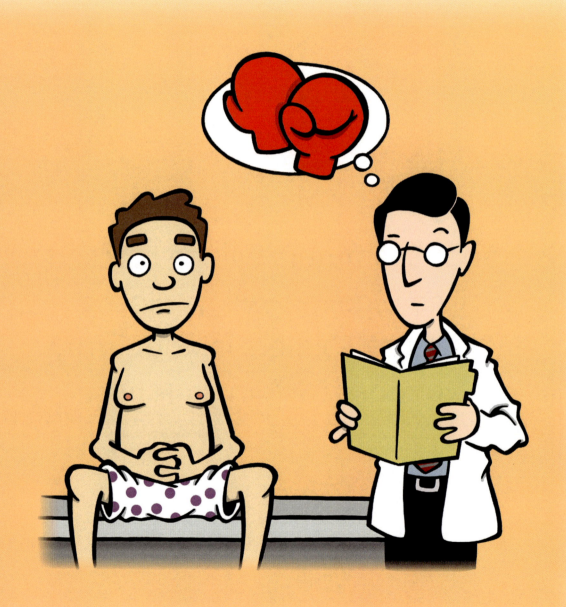

First you'll go to the doctor
For your consultative meeting
And that is when he'll tell you
That your nuts will take a beating

And when the day has come
You will sit down in that chair
And a nurse you've never met before
Will gently shave your hair

Then the doctor will arrive
A moment or two thereafter
And as he snips and makes small talk
You'll fake some awkward laughter

When you leave you'll go home
And think you'll be alright
Until you wake up in the morning
And you'll swear your boys were in a fight

There'll be bruising
There'll be swelling
You'll be sore
You'll be yelling

Just keep the ice pack on it
And be sure to take your meds
Because in a week or two (or three)
You'll get back to action in your bed

Actually that's not right
You first need to be tested
To make sure the surgery was a success
And your swimmers have been bested

So go ahead and get down to it
10 times or more is what you'll need
And then they'll say the pipes are clear
You're free to do the deed

But before you get the go ahead
Not to wrap it when it's up
You'll have to give a sample
In a little plastic cup

And if you're able to get past
The final encounter at reception
Chances are you'll be good to go
For some love sans contraception

Made in the USA
Las Vegas, NV
04 February 2022